A Workbook

Unleash The Power To Complete Your Goals

Six Phases Of Awareness Exercises To Reach Your Objectives

For Health Professionals, Managers and Laypersons

Barbara Warren, Ph.D.
And
Angelika Drake

ISBN: 0-7596-9092-8 (e-book)
ISBN: 0-7596-9093-6 (Paperback)

This book is printed on acid free paper.

I thank my editor, Beverly Bergman for her dedication.

Cover design by: Angelika Drake

QUANTITY PURCHASES

Books are available at special quantity discounts to use as premiums and sales promotions, or for use in corporate training programs, for professional groups, clubs, and other organizations.

For more information, please contact 1stBooks Library at www.1stbooks.com or call 1-888-280-7715.

1stBooks - rev. 04/07/03

DEDICATION

To our mother who knew how to reach her goals and walk on a path of accomplishments.

A Workbook

UNLEASH THE POWER TO COMPLETE YOUR GOALS

Six Phases Of Awareness Exercises To Reach Your Objectives

For Health Professionals,
Managers and Laypersons

Barbara Warren, Ph.D.,
and Angelika Drake

CONTENTS

Phase One: SEE
See, Feel and Allow

Phase Two: STRETCH
Stretch Through the Crosswinds

Phase Three: STAND
Stand Tall to Conquer

Phase Four: TEST
Test Body and Mind

Phase Five: TRAVERSE
Traverse and Master

Phase Six: TRIUMPH
Triumph in the Stretch of Glory

Your Final ANALYSIS
Thoughts About the Workbook

PREFACE

Dr. Barbara Warren and Angelika Drake, the authors, designed these exercises based on their expertise of reaching their own goals as ultra-distance athletes.

The purpose is to heighten the individual's awareness of how to actualize their dreams and desires. The prescription of the Six Phases will give the reader the structure necessary to succeed. It is advisable that you use this personal workbook to discuss it with friends, your coach or counselor. The best way to reach the deeper levels of involvement would be in a workshop guided by a leader who uses this book. Being part of a group can greatly add to the person's motivation. Group participation also leads to the realization that others face similar adversities. The subtle encouragement of others can invoke better results.

As competitive athletes, educators in private practice and motivational seminar leaders, the authors are well aware of some limitations of a workbook. Since the exercises are general, they cannot help every reader in the exact same way. They also advocate that everyone must pay a price for successfully reaching their goals.

There are many goal programs available, but researchers have found that the best way to reach success is through a structured and simplified program that does not need too much time to be implemented. In short, it has to be uncomplicated.

Over the years in their extreme competitions in exotic and remote areas of the world, Angelika and Dr. Barbara have extracted definite lessons so that their own *Completion Of Goals* would surge into reality. Barbara's experience of eighteen years in private practice has added a valuable component of compassion and understanding, which combined with the hands-on experiences, have taught her how to fulfill individual's and the public's expectations.

"We hope that your desires for reaching your dreams will motivate you for possessing a dynamic attitude toward the exercises in the text. You need to actualize your God-given talents to maximize the quality of your life."

INTRODUCTION

For identical twins Angelika and Barbara, living in the status quo has never been an acceptable option. It would be a denial of their God-given blessings, which include both the hard times and the good times, to believe for one second that they cannot do more with what they have been given.

Unleash The Power To Complete Your Goals means knowing how to look inside and finding just one more ounce of effort to attain an objective. In daily life, it can mean many things to different people: facing fears, conquering adversities, starting a new career, losing weight or breaking bad habits, but whatever you decide to take control of, *Unleash The Power To Complete Your Goals* will assist you in achieving your objectives.

The *Goal* philosophy became a major force in the sisters' lives. The subliminal messages are of making decisions and managing risks. This workbook supplies ample exercises that have been applied by the sisters in their own experiences of reaching their many record-winning goals. What they learned has created a clear picture in their minds of the concrete phases necessary for achieving any objective. They recognized that reaching their goals involved going through certain phases over and over—one "race after another," as it were. Soon they found a pattern. Not only did they utilize this pattern for winning in their various athletic events, but they also tested it against the problems and adversities of their daily lives. When reduced to their simplest terms, these awareness exercises translate into a formula for success.

The idea to write this workbook began after Barbara and Angelika had climbed to the summit of one of Northern Italy's Dolomite Mountains. Sitting on top of the world surrounded by fluffy white clouds, they looked back at where they'd just been and realized they'd conquered a difficult challenge. In their glee, they excitedly discussed what each had done to overcome their fears of heights and exhaustion. Both had employed these mental preparation techniques without having ever discussed it with the other. As they rested and talked, it was clear that their thinking was so much alike that both knew with absolute accuracy the phases the other went through to reach that mountaintop. Right there on the pinnacle they formulated the Six Phases of Awareness for reaching their Goals.

Six Phases:

1. See

First you have to See, Feel and Allow your goal to turn into reality. Athletes use this mental preparation for achieving excellence.

2. Stretch

Stretch your physical, mental and spiritual capacities. Problem-solve every step to reach your goals by extending your capacities.

3. Stand

Stand tall above your character, prove your toughness and no matter what keep heading toward the end.

4. Test

In this Phase you will be tested physically, mentally and spiritually. Phase Four is the typical giving-up point. You have come a long way, but there is still more to come and you might be exhausted and stressed. You have to endure this test and keep going until the goal is at hand.

5. Traverse

You have left behind the most difficult parts and from now on you are traversing a manageable territory. People who gave up are missing out on this controllable Phase. In your mind you know you are coming closer to the end, therefore you know that you can endure.

6. Triumph

You are there. You have reached the goal. The business is finished. The award is yours.

All the questionnaires and exercises in the workbook are based on the Six Phases, which need to be completed in sequence. The ordinary problems of life don't require answering the exercises of this workbook because those goals are easy to reach for most individuals. The questionnaires are for handling the "biggies" in your daily life—those problems that appear to be barriers, even though they may seem small or easy to resolve to other people.

Phase One:

SEE

See, Feel and Allow

A TIMELINE ABOUT YOUR LIFE HISTORY

Remember key events and key experiences of your life. See what your life history has to teach you. What were your greatest achievements?

Years	Key Events You Remember
1-9	
9-12	
12-15	
15-18	
18-21	
21-30	
30-40	
40-50	
50-90	

Reflect on the above. How would you describe your life?

- ☐ A drama
- ☐ A melodrama
- ☐ A comedy
- ☐ Or something else?

Describe the Quality of Life you Live Today

YOUR LIFE MAP

Divide your life into different sections.
For example: Family life, business, recreation, goals, your wishes for the future, etc.

☐ From what you know about your life, write down whether you want to leave it as is or change it.

☐ Are there some facts you would like to limit or drop altogether?

☐ Which of your dreams and goals do you still want to fulfill?

Sections of your life:	Do you leave it or do you want to see changes?
1	
2	
3	
4	
5	
6	

SEE, FEEL AND ALLOW YOUR GOALS
Exercise your visualizations

Who Did You Want to Be As a Grown-Up?
Remember your dreams, wishes and desires that you had for your life.

Make a list about:
1. What you actualized
2. What partially happened
3. What never happened

What I Actualized	Partially Happened	Never Happened
1	1	1
2	2	2
3	3	3
4	4	4
5	5	5
6	6	6

☐ What do you still want to accomplish?_____
_____

☐ Who do you want to be?_____
_____

☐ What has held you back in the past and what holds you back now?
_____
_____

Look into Your Future with
See, Feel and Allow

With the power of "See, Feel and Allow," you can create a blueprint that takes you on a voyage into your future. See the big picture and describe it.

In My Mind I Can See My Goals

1. Where I want to go…

2. When I want to get there…

3. The price I am willing to pay is…

4. I want to see a difference in…

See, Feel, Allow and Do Your Goals

Autosuggestion works through creative imagery and fantasy.
Assess what you want to achieve in your life.
Dare to use your dreams for the following exercise:

Four Important Things I Need to Accomplish

1 _____

2 _____

3 _____

4 _____

I See, Feel, Allow and Do...to Achieve (Mental Exercise)

See_____
_____

Feel_____
_____

Allow_____
_____

Do_____
_____

I Will Practice "See, Feel, Allow and Do"
At These Specific Times of the Week:

1_____
2_____
3_____

It Already Happened

Write or talk about your achievements like they have already happened. You can also talk to an imaginary person or write a letter to a person about your success.

My Success Story: My Dreams Came True

FEELINGS CAN TRICK YOUR THINKING

An example of how you change your feelings into rational thinking:

Feelings can talk aloud	Change them into rational thinking
I should look for the most comfortable way to reach my goal.	I accept being uncomfortable in the short run so that I can reach satisfaction and joy in the long run.
If I cannot reach my goals then it shows that I don't have the potential to do so. I am a failure and I feel like a loser.	I will not reach every goal and will not condemn myself for it. I learn from my past and I can move on to new opportunities.
I don't trust myself. Others can do what I cannot do. I feel depressed and lonely.	I will live with my decisions. I will take risks and visualize the unknown so that I can problem-solve solutions.
Others should help me reach my dreams and goals. Without help I feel desperate and abandoned.	I am responsible for reaching beyond my own possible. How far and when I reach it is up to me.
When I feel like approaching my projects it will be the right time to do them.	I am in the ongoing process of learning. My feelings will not dictate my future. My rational thinking (in the present) will create what I want to achieve.

8

11 BELIEFS ABOUT MAKING DECISIONS

1) You have only one choice: make the decision.

2) If you don't decide, there is someone out there that will achieve what you wanted to do.

3) You can make several decisions about your undertaking. Life isn't black and white, all or nothing.

4) You can make a decision without having the perfect answer.

5) You can go ahead with your project even if you cannot eliminate all the risks.

6) Accept that some of your decisions will not synchronize with other people.

7) Don't feel guilt, don't feel like a failure, and don't feel remorseful if you make the wrong decision.

8) Don't decide with your feelings; just do what needs to be done.

9) Visualize the unknown, make it known, and make a decision based on your mental preparation.

10) Don't live or die with every decision; breathe courage into your being and exhale every fear you ever had.

11) When you protect yourself from making a decision, you rob yourself of the many opportunities to succeed.

DECISION-MAKING ASSESSMENT

Answer the following questions quickly and spontaneously:

Whose words/actions are confusing you?
1_____
2_____
3_____

What are your justifications and excuses for not making a decision?
1_____
2_____
3_____

Why are some decisions overwhelming?
1_____
2_____
3_____

Have you set your expectations a little higher than what you can do?
_____

Have you set your expectations lower than your potential?
_____

Have you set your expectations consistently too high?
_____

Are you secretive about your decisions?
_____

What were your greatest successes in decision-making?
1_____
2_____
3_____

To whom did you give the power to derail you from your decisions?
_____
_____

When and why did you feel helpless about making your own decisions?
_____

You are an adult and responsible for the decisions you make. Which ones will you make and which ones do you want to skip? Why would you make or not make them? What is keeping you from making these decisions?
1_____
2_____

WHAT HAVE YOU LEARNED FROM PHASE ONE?

Give a one-sentence conclusion for the following 6 questions:

1. Time line about your life _____

    _____

2. Your life map _____

    _____

3. See, Feel, Allow and Do your goals _____

    _____

4. Who did you want to be as a grown-up _____

    _____

5. Feelings can trick your thinking _____

    _____

6. Phase One decisions _____

    _____

SUMMARY OF PHASE ONE

See, Feel, Allow and Do

List 2 or 3 projects you have always wanted to actualize:

1_____

_____

_____

_____

2_____

_____

_____

_____

3_____

_____

_____

_____

Describe how you SEE your future

Phase Two:

STRETCH

Stretch Through the Crosswinds

CROSSWINDS AND MENTAL TOUGHNESS
Without mental toughness you cannot make it through Phase Two.

Mental Toughness Is Learned, Not Inherited

How did your parents model mental toughness to you when you grew up?

_____

_____

What did teachers or other mentors show you about mental toughness?

_____

_____

How much mental toughness do you use in your life?

_____

How much more mental toughness would you like to have?

_____

Do you search out opportunities that can teach you about mental toughness?

_____

_____

How courageous are you to embrace tough situations?

_____

_____

What were the two most outstanding circumstances where you used mental toughness?

1_____

2_____

Does mental toughness translate into consistency in your life?

_____

_____

THE CROSSWINDS CHECKLIST

Crosswinds means adversities, hardships and obstacles, which you encounter in
Phase Two

Answer from I to 10: 1 being the least and 10 the most:

Can you be positive but still realistic?
1   2   3   4   5   6   7   8   9   10

Are you managing your emotions in crosswind instances?
1   2   3   4   5   6   7   8   9   10

Can you be calm and relaxed in demanding moments?
1   2   3   4   5   6   7   8   9   10

Can you be energetic and ready for action?
1   2   3   4   5   6   7   8   9   10

Is your determination strong enough in spite of the crosswinds?
1   2   3   4   5   6   7   8   9   10

Can you be mentally alert and stay focused?
1   2   3   4   5   6   7   8   9   10

How confident are you when confronted by complex tasks?
1   2   3   4   5   6   7   8   9   10

Do you take full responsibility for your actions?
1   2   3   4   5   6   7   8   9   10

Are the adversities (crosswinds) in your life too much to handle?
1   2   3   4   5   6   7   8   9   10

How hard do the crosswinds of your life hit you?
1   2   3   4   5   6   7   8   9   10

How well do you cope with your crosswinds?
1   2   3   4   5   6   7   8   9   10

Your Battle Against The Crosswinds

Have you experienced being your own toughest opponent?

Yes _____Sometimes _____Never

Do you handle the crosswinds that are between you and your goal?

Yes _____Sometimes _____Never

Do you believe that winning is 75% mental?

Yes _____Maybe _____No

Do you concentrate on winning the contest with yourself?

Yes _____Sometimes _____Never

Do you experience the conquest of self in a consistent manner?

Yes _____Sometimes _____No

Do conflicts scare you?

Yes _____Sometimes _____Never

Do you avoid disagreement?

Yes _____Sometimes _____Never

Do you give up things in order to achieve a higher goal?

Yes _____Sometimes _____Never

Do you succeed with yourself on a daily basis?

Yes _____Sometimes _____Never

PATTERNS OF AVOIDANCE

Which avoidance patterns do you use?

When do you use these patterns?

With whom do you use them?

	Frequently	Seldom	With Whom
Procrastinate			
Distract			
Divert			
Postpone			
Hold back			
Suppress			
Hesitate			
Withhold			
Reschedule			
Interrupt			
Break up			
Suspend			

VALUES FOR PHASE TWO EXPERIENCES

In Phase Two the crosswinds can shatter your beliefs if your values are not grounded solidly. **Translate Your Values into Positive Actions.**

☐ Needs are concrete and physical
☐ **Values are abstract and linked to meanings**
☐ People can compromise their needs
☐ **People do not change their values**
☐ Needs are specific and instant
☐ **Values are lasting; they are your fundamental beliefs**

Value Assessment

Some of the values for my life are:
How my values give meaning to my life:
How my values help me through the crosswinds:
The way I express my values:
How I use my values with other people:
How I see others express their values:

YOUR COMFORT ZONE AND THE SUCCESS LADDER

First Step:
Positive self-image

How do you stretch yourself to obtain a great self-image?

Second Step:
Positive attitude

Do you continuously stretch toward a positive attitude?

Third Step:
Optimistic Expectations

Do you stretch your expectations toward optimistic goals?

Fourth Step:
Responsible behaviors

Do you stretch your behaviors so they display absolute responsibility?

Fifth Step:
Peak performances

Do you stretch yourself to reach peak performances?

STRETCH YOURSELF OPTIMISTICALLY

March through the crosswinds with confidence

Circle the numbers 1 to 4 with:

    1. Almost always   3. Seldom
    2. Sometimes   4. Almost never

I know how to stretch myself to reach my goals.
    1   2   3   4

I can stretch myself so I don't get distracted or lose my focus.
    1   2   3   4

I see myself as a peak performer.
    1   2   3   4

I can stretch myself to handle large amounts of stress.
    1   2   3   4

I want to work hard and pay the price for achieving success.
    1   2   3   4

I am able to proceed with my projects with passion even
when I face difficult problems.
    1   2   3   4

My self-talk during stretching my capacities is positive.
    1   2   3   4

When I make mistakes, I stretch even further to reach my goal.
    1   2   3   4

I can stretch to work at the upper range of my talents most of the time.
    1   2   3   4

I don't think of missed opportunities and past mistakes.
    1   2   3   4

I get challenged and inspired in difficult situations.
      1   2   3   4

I project an image of a confident person.
      1   2   3   4

I wake up in the morning wanting to stretch my potential.
      1   2   3   4

I can turn adversities into new possibilities.
      1   2   3   4

I can be relaxed in the midst of my circumstances.
      1   2   3   4

I have the capacity to adapt quickly to new situations.
      1   2   3   4

When situations are overwhelming, I like the way I cope.
      1   2   3   4

Life experiences have humbled me but they have not made me angry.
      1   2   3   4

I have used the power of my faith to overcome obstacles.
      1   2   3   4

☐ Use a colored pencil to draw a line from the first number you have circled to the second and third, through all the numbers all the way down to the last.

☐ By the shape of your colored line, you will see how positive you are.
Maybe you tend to be in the middle or all the way to the right, which indicates a negative approach for reaching your goals.
Maybe you zigzag, which means that you are positive in certain areas but not in all of them.

☐ Learn how to lean toward the left side of the exercise sheet and note the areas in which you can improve.

EXERCISE STRETCHING YOUR COMFORT ZONE

Write a brief statement describing 3 or 4 ways that you can stretch yourself. Then support each of those areas/goals by responding to the subsequent questions using 1 line for each of the corresponding 4 goals.

In what areas of your life do you desire to stretch?
1_____
2_____
3_____

What is the purpose?
1_____
2_____
3_____

When will you start?
1_____
2_____
3_____

How will you do it?
1_____
2_____
3_____

What will people say or think about you?
1_____
2_____
3_____

How will you feel about yourself *after* having stretched your comfort zone?
1_____
2_____
3_____

Go over these main points with people that are close to you and discuss what you have learned.

WHAT HAVE YOU LEARNED FROM PHASE TWO?

Give a one-sentence conclusion for the following 4 questions:

1. Describe the crosswinds of your life and your mental toughness.

   _____

   _____

2. Describe your patterns of avoidance.

   _____

   _____

3. What have you learned from your success ladder?

   _____

   _____

4. What have you learned about stretching your comfort zone?

   _____

   _____

SUMMARY OF PHASE TWO

Stretch Through The Crosswinds

Give three statements to show how you are going to
use your mental toughness, overcome your avoidance
mechanisms, and be ready to pay the price.

1_____

_____

_____

2_____

_____

_____

3_____

_____

_____

_____

Write into the design about how you are going to STRTECH yourself

Phase Three:

STAND

Stand Tall to Conquer

STAND TALL TO BUILD YOUR CHARACTER

In this Phase you will encounter even more frustrations and stress. You can stand tall through your adversities because you know a reward waits at the end.

Respond to the open-ended questions by filling in the sentences:

I can stand tall above my character when…

When I choose character-building opportunities I…

Standing tall in spite of criticism, rejections and mistakes is…

I want to stand tall above my circumstances because…

When others see me standing tall they…

The consequences for standing tall in my life will be…

Moving through the Third Phase makes me feel…

My models for standing tall in life…

I want to be able to stand as tall as…

By standing tall I am…

Stand Tall Above Pain

1. **Chosen pain**:   You choose to endure this pain
2. **Unhealthy pain**:   Childhood, environment, circumstances
3. **Unavoidable pain**:   Accidents, dying, sicknesses
4. **Self-inflicted pain**: As in a mental illness

Fill all the boxes with numbers from 0 to 3, with 0 being the least and 3 being the strongest sense of pain. You might feel a little of one pain, and some of the other pains. Use a different color for each number (ex. 0=red, 1=blue…)

	Chosen pain	Unhealthy pain	Unavoidable pain	Self-inflicted pain
When I confront a stressful Phase 3 experience, I feel…	Example 3	2	0	1
When under stress, the physical symptoms of my pain appear as…				
Messages from my childhood cause…				
My passions for risky endeavors cause me to…				
My life has been filled with…				
My undertakings cause me…				
I had accidents and sicknesses that caused…				
I want to risk and accept…				
I embrace my circumstances and feel…				
In the future I want to choose…				

☐ Look at the configuration by connecting like-color numbers and analyze your pain pattern.

☐ Work on what needs to be changed by using the 6 Phases to make you strong.

CONQUER

Conquer Your Frustrations

The easy approach to pleasure and fun is usually less rewarding than the more difficult path.

Agree	Disagree	Sometimes	Maybe	I want to change
❏	❏	❏	❏	❏

I am happiest when I am involved in challenges that make me act against idleness and lethargy.

Agree	Disagree	Sometimes	Maybe	I want that
❏	❏	❏	❏	❏

I don't like to do certain things but I do them because they get very complicated if I delay.

Agree	Disagree	Sometimes	Maybe	I want to change
❏	❏	❏	❏	❏

It might not be fair that I have to work so hard but my life does not have to be easy.

Agree	Disagree	Sometimes	Maybe	I want the easy way out
❏	❏	❏	❏	❏

To arrive at good results, many times I have to do things I don't like to do.

Agree	Disagree	Sometimes	Maybe	I don't want to
❏	❏	❏	❏	❏

I really don't like to become frustrated but I can handle it reasonably well.

Agree	Disagree	Sometimes	Maybe	I don't like it
❏	❏	❏	❏	❏

Conquer Your Circumstances

Answer by circling 1 for the least and 10 for the most:

Can you be tough when the circumstances are difficult?

    1   2   3   4   5   6   7   8   9   10

Can you conquer most of your frustrations?

    1   2   3   4   5   6   7   8   9   10

Can you smoothly conquer difficult people's agendas?

    1   2   3   4   5   6   7   8   9   10

Can you conquer your own impulsiveness?

    1   2   3   4   5   6   7   8   9   10

Can you delay gratification?

    1   2   3   4   5   6   7   8   9   10

Can you conquer the temptations of pleasures?

    1   2   3   4   5   6   7   8   9   10

Can you conquer your anger?

    1   2   3   4   5   6   7   8   9   10

Can you conquer your fears?

    1   2   3   4   5   6   7   8   9   10

Can you conquer negative messages from your past?

    1   2   3   4   5   6   7   8   9   10

Can you conquer distractions that stop you from reaching your goal?

    1   2   3   4   5   6   7   8   9   10

☐ Write a one-sentence explanation below every row of numbers.

☐ What do you most need to conquer, change or modify so that you can successfully reach the end of your undertakings?

TURN YOUR ADVERSITIES INTO CHALLENGES

Challenge Awareness Exercise

Answer with your creative mind and list all the solutions you possibly think of:

1. Go back in time and remember one of the opportunities you missed.
    How would you handle the same situation today? _____

2. Are you tough enough to endure your situation until completion, no matter what? _____

3. State four creative ideas how you would turn a specific adversity into a challenge. _____

4. Using a real situation, explain how you could or could not turn an adversity into a challenge. _____

5. Have you seen other people turning adversities into challenges? How did they do it? _____

6. Do you search out challenges so that you can practice your skills to overcome the adversities that come with it? _____

7. List the adversities that you have turned into opportunities in your life. _____

8. What can you still do about those you were not successful with, and when will you start? _____

9. How would you feel about yourself if you could turn most of your adversities into great challenges? _____

10. How will you tolerate frustrations, and challenge yourself in outstanding and new ways? _____

STAND TALL TO CONQUER THE THIRD PHASE
8 Guidelines for Phase Three
Circle what leads you to conquer Phase Three:

1. Will you **Think of** how to stand tall and conquer when needed? YES ➔ I HOPE ➔ NO ➔

2. Will you **Practice** to handle your frustrations in crucial moments? YES ➔ I HOPE ➔ NO ➔

3. Can you **Implement** what needs to be done to reach your goals? YES ➔ I HOPE ➔ NO ➔

4. Can you consistently **Move** forward to carry out your plans? YES ➔ I HOPE ➔ NO ➔

5. Can you easily **Tolerate** difficult circumstances? YES ➔ I HOPE ➔ NO ➔

6. Will you **Stand Tall** all the way through until you reach your dream? YES ➔ I HOPE ➔ NO ➔

7. Can you **Conquer** every inch of your problems most of the time? YES ➔ I HOPE ➔ NO ➔

8. Do you **Ask for and believe in God's** wisdom, guidance and power? YES ➔ I HOPE ➔ NO ➔

Results: Circle the total number of times you answered "yes," "I hope," and "no."

How Many	"YES"	Do You Have?	1 2 3 4 5 6 7 8
How Many	"I HOPE"	Do You Have?	1 2 3 4 5 6 7 8
How Many	"NO"	Do You Have?	1 2 3 4 5 6 7 8

YES
Means you are ready, committed and willing to pay the price.

I HOPE
Means that you are wavering in the nowhere zone, not getting anywhere, only hoping but not doing.

NO
Means you might be rebellious or have a fear of the unknown, anxieties about succeeding, or problems from your past.

WHAT HAVE YOU LEARNED FROM PHASE THREE?

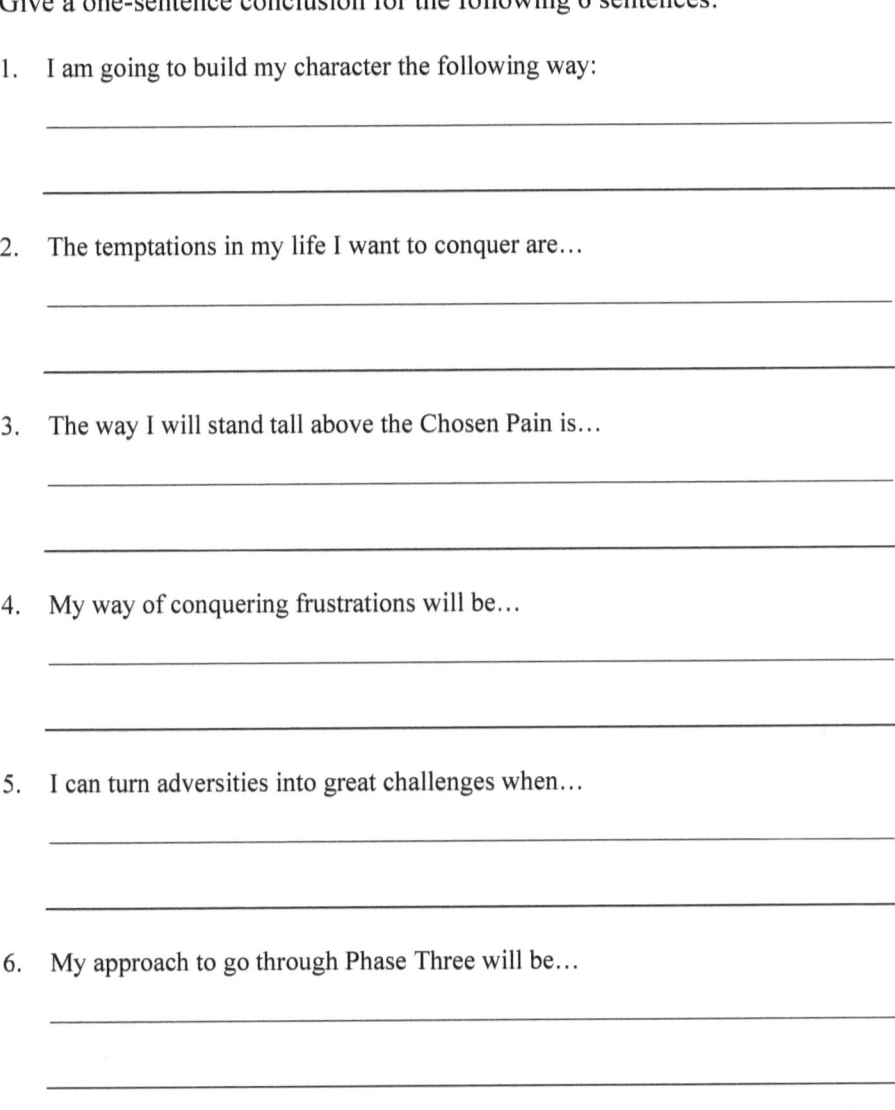

Give a one-sentence conclusion for the following 6 sentences:

1. I am going to build my character the following way:

   _____

   _____

2. The temptations in my life I want to conquer are…

   _____

   _____

3. The way I will stand tall above the Chosen Pain is…

   _____

   _____

4. My way of conquering frustrations will be…

   _____

   _____

5. I can turn adversities into great challenges when…

   _____

   _____

6. My approach to go through Phase Three will be…

   _____

   _____

SUMMARY OF PHASE THREE

Stand Tall to Conquer

Give Three Ways That You Will Stand Tall And Conquer Your
Circumstances:

1 _____

_____

_____

2 _____

_____

_____

3 _____

_____

_____

Write about your ways to STAND tall in life.

Phase Four:

TEST

Test Body and Mind

GIVING UP VERSUS GOING ON

Look for a pattern in you life that points toward giving up on your projects or opportunities. Or look for a pattern that shows that you can follow through to reach your goals sometimes, or one that indicates that you never give up.

Your Life Pattern

Circle whichever applies to you:

I easily give up when the pressure becomes too much	Give up	Sometimes	Never
When the demands or expectations are too high I…	Give up	Sometimes	Never
When I feel uncomfortable I…	Give up	Sometimes	Never
Personal confrontations make me…	Give up	Sometimes	Never
Projects that last too long make me…	Give up	Sometimes	Never
When in any kind of pain I…	Give up	Sometimes	Never
When I have too many projects to accomplish I…	Give up	Sometimes	Never
When I don't know where to begin I…	Give up	Sometimes	Never
Once I reach a Fourth Phase experience, I am too worn out to go any further and…	Give up	Sometimes	Never
When toughness counts I…	Give up	Sometimes	Never
When I believe the outcome will not be successful I…	Give up	Sometimes	Never
My emotions dictate when to…	Give up	Sometimes	Never
The pattern in my life is to…	Give up	Sometimes	Never

Are you content with the above pattern? _____

What would you like to change? _____

Giving up has no destination. Toughness is a voyage with a finish.
One voyage follows another with no end.

PHASE FOUR AWARENESS

Are you aware of the Phase Four experiences in your life, the typical 'giving-up' moments?   Yes   No

If you use your thinking more than your feelings, do you believe that you can change from giving up to getting going?   Yes   No

If you use the potentials of your body, mind and soul in superior ways, do you believe you will pass to Phase Five?   Yes   No

Have you set your goals too high or have you planned for too many?   Yes   No

Has giving up usually been an option in your life?   Yes   No

Have you had authority figures that modeled a giving-up lifestyle for you?   Yes   No

Have you had any traumatic incident or other emotional experiences that caused you to have a giving-up lifestyle?   Yes   No

BODY, MIND AND SOUL POTENTIAL

Your body, mind and soul will be tested in Phase Four. Many people give up at this point because their body, mind and soul potentials are not strong enough.

Test Your Mind Potential

Circle your answer:

Are you continuously acquiring new information?
      I do   I don't

Are you daydreaming toward the completion of your goals?
      I do   I don't

Are you daydreaming to escape reality?
      I do   I don't

Do you fantasize about your success without its actualization?
      I do   I don't

Are you doing something about new and old wishes?
      I do   I don't

Do you plan your day and week?
      I do   I don't

Do you plan your month and year?
      I do   I don't

Do you organize your chores or projects before you start?
      I do   I don't

Does your self-talk (inner voice) say that you will reach your goals?
      It does   It doesn't

Do you continuously problem-solve using your creativity?
        I do   I don't

Can you learn and recall easily?
        I do   I don't

Do you calculate and classify (analytical logical thinking) without difficulty?
        I do   I don't

Do you think toward your specific goals, finding specific solutions?
        I do   I don't

Do you structure your life enough for getting things done?
        I do   I don't

Do you challenge your thinking capacities with difficult tasks?
        I do   I don't

Assessment of the Exercise

1. Count how many times you answered "I do" and "I don't." Fifty percent of "I do" or "I don't" places you in the middle ground without going anywhere.

2. If you answered "I don't" more than five times you need to make a serious effort to pass through Phase Four, otherwise you cannot reach Phase Five and you cannot experience the stretch of glory that comes with finishing difficult tasks.

3. If you circled "I do" more than six times you still need to make an effort but you are on your way into Phase Five, which leads you to traverse that stretch to embrace your goal.

Test Your Body Potential

Describe your body type:

1. Endomorphic: Thick bones, wide hips, gains weight easily, slow metabolism

2. Ectomorphic: Long and slender build, light bone structure, narrow shoulders and hips, high metabolism

3. Mesomorphic: Medium bone structure, shoulders wider than hips, slender waist and hips, low body fat, neither slow nor fast metabolism

Health and Body Strength

Describe which body type you are:

_____

To achieve your goals successfully you need a strong body. How much have you invested in your health and body strength?

_____

Is your lifestyle geared toward health and high performance?

_____

What are the activities that make you physically powerful?

_____

Is your nutrition balanced enough to make you strong and healthy?

_____

Do you have the structure and discipline that create your body's potential to be exceptional?

_____

Do you sometimes go beyond your own possible to test your body's potential?
If so, what do you do?

_____

How high of a price are you willing to pay to have a healthy and solid body?

_____

Do you routinely test the strength, endurance and flexibility of your body?

_____

Test Your Soul Potential

Your soul is the invisible part of you. It contains your moral or emotional nature, thinking, understanding, courage, love, honor and your spiritual beliefs.

Search Your Soul

List 3 ways you search your soul:
1_____
2_____
3_____

Explain 3 ways you cultivate the integrity (thinking and feeling parts) of your soul:
1_____
2_____
3_____

What have your spiritual beliefs been and what are they now?
1_____
2_____
3_____

Do you test your soul potential by your values? If so, what are they?
1_____
2_____
3_____

Are there temptations in your life that make you weak?
1_____
2_____
3_____

In what ways do you consciously empower the invisible part of you, your soul?
1_____
2_____
3_____

How do you manage your emotions to strengthen your soul?
1_____
2_____
3_____

Share the results with your group or people close to you. Tell them what you can still modify or change to test your soul.

BODY, MIND AND SOUL
TESTED BY STRESS
Selected Stress is essential to growth and leads to improvement
in the appropriate areas.

Selected Stress Exercise

When you choose your project or event you will also embrace a certain amount of stress that parallels your undertaking. You select this kind of stress and will manage it with awareness. Your body, mind and soul will be tested.

(Yes)   (No)   I am very good at choosing projects that teach me to handle the Selected Stress.

(Yes)   (No)   I have a hard time coping with any stressful situation.

(Yes)   (No)   I deal well with stress in certain areas but not in others.

(Yes)   (No)   I handle physical stress better than emotional stress.

(Yes)   (No)   Stress has helped me to focus, concentrate and meet my challenges (Selected Stress).

(Yes)   (No)   My Selected Stress stems from a positive cause, other stress snowballs from negative causes and I will try to avoid it.

(Yes)   (No)   Changes in my life are the source of major stress.

(Yes)   (No)   My positive reaction to the Selected Stress causes enthusiasm, increased productivity and a zest for life.

(Yes)   (No)   When stress overwhelms me I feel persistent anxiety, fatigue, insomnia, irritability, dizzy spells, indecisiveness, depression, guilt, remorse.

(Yes)   (No)   I cannot get rid of all my stress but I can learn how to live with it.

10 Stress Crashers

1. Recognize the stress "warning" signs. Relax immediately. Let your feelings talk to you and problem-solve a solution.

2. Acknowledge your peak stresses and handle one item at a time.

3. Prevent breakdowns by inviting down time into your life.

4. Be in tune with body, mind and soul, and give each what they need.

5. Don't project your stress onto others; learn to change your attitude and circumstance for a while until you feel better again.

6. Learn to accept and adapt to unpleasant changes.

7. Keep up with your health: Sleep, exercise and diet.

8. Relaxation tapes and exercises help eliminate stress.

9. Sometimes a total change of lifestyle alleviates stress.

10. Choose projects that guide you through the Six Phases and you will forget about the regular stress.

GO THROUGH PHASE FOUR AGGRESSIVELY

Learn to actualize the terms that follow and write one or two words that convey what they mean to you.

You need a certain fierceness to pass through Phase Four.

---

1. Prevail   _____
2. Triumph   _____
3. Overcome   _____
4. Rise above   _____
5. Capture   _____
6. Succeed   _____
7. Overpower   _____
8. Dominate   _____
9. Rule over   _____
10. Control   _____
11. Take over   _____
12. Press on   _____
13. Speed up   _____
14. No pause   _____
15. Move up   _____
16. Test   _____

Which are the words you use to stretch through Phase Four?
☐ Place a yellow mark next to them

Which are the ones you have never used?
☐ Place a blue mark next to them

Which ones do you want to use in the future?
☐ Place a red mark next to them

Are you satisfied with what you see?_____
What do you want to change? _____

DRIVE DISCERNMENT
Body and mind continually need to be supplied with forces that drive you forward.

A Drive Discernment Profile
Answer with 10 to 1, from the highest to the lowest level you operate under, only choosing one word from each line (either left or right side).

Motivated	10 9 8 7 6 5 4 3 2 1	Unprovoked
Aggressive	10 9 8 7 6 5 4 3 2 1	Fragile
Courage	10 9 8 7 6 5 4 3 2 1	Spineless
Energetic	10 9 8 7 6 5 4 3 2 1	Sluggish
Resilient	10 9 8 7 6 5 4 3 2 1	Rigid
Determent	10 9 8 7 6 5 4 3 2 1	Reluctant
Activate	10 9 8 7 6 5 4 3 2 1	Paralyzed
Vigor	10 9 8 7 6 5 4 3 2 1	Weak
Discipline	10 9 8 7 6 5 4 3 2 1	Self-indulgent
Aspiration	10 9 8 7 6 5 4 3 2 1	Boredom
Passion	10 9 8 7 6 5 4 3 2 1	Indifferent
Inspired	10 9 8 7 6 5 4 3 2 1	Dull
Enthusiastic	10 9 8 7 6 5 4 3 2 1	Apathetic
Intense	10 9 8 7 6 5 4 3 2 1	Moderate

Drive Discernment Profile Results

☐ Draw a colored line between the points you have marked and look at the graph that appears. The more you are to the left the easier it will be to reach all your goals.

☐ If your graph leans to the right you know that urgent work needs to be done for a better quality of life.

☐ If it is in the middle, then you might not be a high achiever. You are not a loser but not a winner either.

The Drive Discernment factors can change through awareness.
They are not permanent.
They are acquired patterns of thinking and behaving that have a profound consequence on your ability to reach your goals.

RISK-TAKING ABILITY TEST

Solid risks are measured risks. Radical risks are impulsive and not thought through. You choose solid risks by choosing goals you want to achieve.

Solid Risks

(Yes) (No) 1. Do you stop yourself from taking risks because of what others might think?

(Yes) (No) 2. Do you prefer security to excitement?

(Yes) (No) 3. Do you seek contentment over passion?

(Yes) (No) 4. Do you want a low-key life compared to a driven lifestyle?

(Yes) (No) 5. Are you afraid you won't measure up?

(Yes) (No) 6. Does fear of failure hold you back?

(Yes) (No) 7. Do you plan ahead so your risks are measured and solid?

(Yes) (No) 8. Do you look forward to the challenge of solid risks?

(Yes) (No) 9. Can you remain calm when confronted with a solid risk?

(Yes) (No) 10. Do you evaluate the consequences of the risks you take?

(Yes) (No) 11. Do you consider the timing for the solid risk?

(Yes) (No) 12. Do you hang around other solid-risk takers?

(Yes) (No) 13. Have you been a successful solid-risk taker in your past?

(Yes) (No) 14. Do you back off at the first sign of failures?

(Yes) (No) 15. Do you think security and safety exist in nature?

(Yes) (No) 16. Do you look for opportunities to test your risk-taking abilities?

(Yes) (No) 17. Have you taken impulsive radical risks too often?

Write down how many (Yes) and (No) answers you have:

(Yes)   (No)

Write Down Four Statements About The Above 17 Answers

Make your own analysis:

1 _____
_____

2 _____
_____

3 _____
_____

4 _____
_____

What are you going to do about your findings?

1 _____
_____

2 _____
_____

3 _____
_____

1 _____
_____

LEARNING AND PERFORMING

Stretch body, mind and soul by learning and performing.

1. The door opener for improving your performance is to understand what role your mind plays in your successes and failures. Do you have your mind set for winning performances?

_____

_____

2. Great performers believe in themselves and express it with courage. Express your own beliefs about your success and failures:

_____

_____

3. You act according to the pictures engraved in your mind. Your performance is consistent with these images. Do you see successes or failures? If you see failures, do you know where they stem from, and are you willing to change them?

_____

_____

4. By learning, you are going to stretch your body, mind and soul. If you were a rubber band, how much resistance would you endure before snapping?

_____

_____

5. "Selected Stress" and "Chosen Pain" are part of learning and performing. Are you willing to live with both?

_____

_____

6. Giving up means going half way to your goal. Using the strength of your body, mind and soul leads to complete performances. Have you had mostly half or complete performances in your life?

_____

_____

7. There are Six Phases to reach your goals. What are they?

SE ....   TE....................................
STR.................................   TRA..................................
STA ....   TRI ....

WHAT HAVE YOU LEARNED FROM PHASE FOUR?

Mental beliefs and giving up

_____

_____

Opportunities to test body, mind and soul

_____

Selected Stress

_____

Drive and ambition

_____

Learning and performing

_____

_____

SUMMARY OF PHASE FOUR

Test your body and mind potential

Give three statements about what you will do to avoid giving up.

1_____

_____

_____

2_____

_____

_____

3_____

_____

_____

_____

Write about how you are going to TEST yourself

Phase Five:

TRAVERSE

Traverse and Master

TRAVERSE

You have made it through the toughest stretch, Phase Four.
Now you are mastering your task as you traverse safe and sound through the
Fifth Phase.

Your personal experience:

Traversing means that most of the adversities of your undertaking are placed behind
you.
Portray the significance of traversing toward your goal in the space below:

How many times in your life have you had these experiences? How many more
would you like to have?

Have you usually been on your own, or were you involved with others when you
traversed Phase Five?

Assess the value and purpose of a Phase Five traversing experience:

MASTERY IS CREATED

Talent and Mastery Assessment

List which of your talents you have actualized in your life:

1_____ 2_____ 3_____ 4_____

5_____ 6_____ 7_____ 8_____

List those talents you have seen actualized in your family:

1_____ 2_____ 3_____ 4_____

5_____ 6_____ 7_____ 8_____

Describe how long it took you to master each of your talents: days, months or years?

1_____ 2_____ 3_____ 4_____

5_____ 6_____ 7_____ 8_____

List any talents you still want to master in your life:

1_____ 2_____ 3_____ 4_____

5_____ 6_____ 7_____ 8_____

Express the feelings you would experience when you create and master your undertakings:

1_____ 2_____ 3_____ 4_____

5_____ 6_____ 7_____ 8_____

What would you lose if you never created and mastered each of your talents?

1_____ 2_____ 3_____ 4_____

5_____ 6_____ 7_____ 8_____

What creative qualities have others seen in you?

1_____ 2_____ 3_____ 4_____

5_____ 6_____ 7_____ 8_____

TRAVERSE YOUR OWN LANDSCAPE

Creativity is subjective and free. Your expression can only be yours and no one else's in the world.

Use Your Emotions to Draw Your Landscape:

A. Draw a beautiful Phase Five landscape while you picture yourself **traversing** the hills, the planes and the fields that take you to your goal. How does it look? Do you run, walk, rest, stand, pray or do something else?

B. Put yourself into the scenery and feel the **emotions** of mastering your undertaking. Make a drawing about your feelings with colored pencils.

C. How much do you like what you see? What would you like to **change**? Visualize what this would look like and draw it below.

COMMITMENT, DISCIPLINE
AND CONSISTENCY (CDC)
These are all vital concepts to developing great character

The CDC Check List:

☐ To check your commitment, discipline and consistency, circle the number that best corresponds to your attitude regarding the two following opposite statements.

5 = strongly agree   4 = agree somewhat   3 = neutral
2 = disagree somewhat   1 = strongly disagree

The three concepts will be referred to as CDC.

I view CDC as an opportunity, not a threat. I should use more techniques to achieve better CDC.	5 4 3 2 1 5 4 3 2 1	I reject CDC and consider it a personal threat. If forced to use more CDC I openly would be more hostile.
A reorganization of my lifestyle would be welcome.	5 4 3 2 1 5 4 3 2 1	I would hate any reorganization. I resist changes that ask for CDC.
I am good at CDC but I can still improve.	5 4 3 2 1 5 4 3 2 1	I am not good at CDC and I have never known how to do it.
New assignments to test my CDC excite me.	5 4 3 2 1 5 4 3 2 1	New assignments intimidate my CDC.

I am motivated by the high expectations of CDC in today's world.	5 4 3 2 1 5 4 3 2 1	I wish that I had lived 200 years ago when life was simpler.
I know that the capacity of my CDC enables me to reach all my goals.	5 4 3 2 1 5 4 3 2 1	CDC robs me of feeling good.
I want to make CDC my companion for life.	5 4 3 2 1 5 4 3 2 1	It is almost impossible to integrate CDC into my lifestyle.
CDC makes me feel confident and powerful.	5 4 3 2 1 5 4 3 2 1	I was too hurt in childhood to be able to use CDC.
Other people intimidate my CDC capacities.	5 4 3 2 1 5 4 3 2 1	I am ashamed and guilty about not using CDC.
With joy I will climb mental and physical mountains using CDC.	5 4 3 2 1 5 4 3 2 1	I am emotionally drained or physically too sick to use CDC in my life.

TOTAL FOR EACH COLUMN: ☐ ☐

☐ High scores in the first column show that you are committed, have discipline, and are consistent. You should handle the Six Phases easily.

☐ High scores in the second column indicate that you need to do a number of Phase One to Six experiences so that you can stretch beyond your own possible. That way you will practice and achieve CDC, which then makes it easier to reach your goals.

SURVIVAL POWER

Deep within you exists a powerful instinct for survival that assists you through all adversities of life. Your adrenal glands produce the hormone adrenaline for fight and flight instincts that will be released in moments of need.

Endurance

Answer with one sentence each of the following questions:

I.   How do you measure up when great obstacles pile up in front of you?

---

2.   Are you patient enough so that your hormones for fight can be released?

---

3.   What do you understand by survival power?

---

4.   Next time a difficult situation comes up can you get in touch with your survival power and let your hormones take over?

---

5.   Have you ever been aware of, or have you ever used, your survival power?

---

6.   Your hormones need an outlet. They exist for the purpose of being used. Do you invite enough exciting situations to release them?

---

7.   Selected Stress and the Chosen Pain are healthy means to feed your survival power. Are you ready to let your hormones strive?

Write a one-sentence summary about your survival power awareness:

WHAT HAVE YOU LEARNED FROM PHASE FIVE?

Give a one-sentence conclusion for each of the following 5 questions:

1. What have you learned about how to successfully traverse Phase Five for your future?

    _____

    _____

2. How have you created mastery in your life and how will you go about it in the future?

    _____

    _____

3. How are you going to actualize your fantasy drawing about traversing the landscape of your life?

    _____

    _____

4. Explain your responsibility toward Commitments, Discipline and Consistency (CDC).

    _____

    _____

5. Search for survival power experiences because they can be healthy for your body. What do you have in mind?

    _____

    _____

SUMMARY OF PHASE FIVE

Traverse and Master:

List 2 or 3 future projects that you will undertake so that you can gain Phase Five experiences:

1 _____

_____

_____

2 _____

_____

_____

3 _____

_____

_____

_____

Write about how you imagine to TRAVERSE your last obstacles

Phase Six:

TRIUMPH

Triumph in the Stretch of Glory

SELF-ASSESSMENT

Answer each question with your knowledge of the Phases you have passed through:

1. Have you had many experiences finishing your undertakings with outstanding success?

    _____

    _____

    _____

2. List the most important ones:

    _____

    _____

    _____

3. How did you feel at the end of each of your accomplishments?

    _____

    _____

    _____

4. Who else was usually involved? Or are you a solo achiever?

    _____

    _____

    _____

5. What was the reaction from other people about your success?

    _____

    _____

    _____

6. Do you usually leave completed projects behind you?

_____

_____

_____

7. How much effort is it to get to the end of your endeavors?

_____

_____

_____

8. Do you want to do it again many more times over?

_____

_____

_____

9. Which one is usually the hardest Phase for you?

_____

_____

_____

10. Which one can you conquer the easiest?

_____

_____

_____

11. With the awareness of the Six Phases can you clearly see a pattern to go beyond your own expectations?

_____

_____

_____

12. What decisions have you made for your future?

_____

_____

_____

AN OVERVIEW OF YOUR WORK

Use the keywords to reach your goals:

- ☐ How are you going to apply the Six Phases in the future?
- ☐ Use three of your major goals for practicing this exercise.
- ☐ Go through every Phase applying the six keywords as they apply to your goals:

1.	SEE	for Phase	1
2.	STRETCH	for Phase	2
3.	STAND	for Phase	3
4.	TEST	for Phase	4
5.	TRAVERSE	for Phase	5
6.	TRIUMPH	for Phase	6

Phase One
1 _____
2 _____
3 _____

Phase Two
1 _____
2 _____
3 _____

Phase Three
1 _____
2 _____
3 _____

Phase Four
1 _____
2 _____
3 _____

Phase Five
1 _____
2 _____
3 _____

Phase Six
1 _____
2 _____
3 _____

At which Phase could you get stuck?
Which Phase would be the easiest for you to go through?
Which Phase do you need to work on the most?

YOUR 10 WINNING GOAL ACTIONS

Because of your actions you have made it all the way to the last Phase.
A positive self-talk is necessary for the successful completion of your desires.

Here are 10 reminders why you have come this far:

1. Because of my goals, my thoughts have crystallized and they have provoked me to strong actions.

2. My goals have kept me focused and have facilitated my problem-solving skills.

3. I have achieved many goals and because of it I am a peak performer.

4. Once I got started and got going, I became like a torpedo that was launched and had no return.

5. My goals have taught me structure and that I could tailor the element of time successfully into my expectations.

6. I have refined my skills and talents through the process of the Six Phases and I will polish them to even greater satisfaction.

7. I have reached for attainable goals but I also have stretched to reach further.

8. I was capable of keeping my goal in sight at all times. I knew how to manage distractions.

9. My mistakes were never big enough so that I would quit.

10. I have not only fulfilled my goals but I will also better them.

TRIUMPH IN THE STRETCH OF GLORY

The stretch of glory crowns you with the greatest gift to build your character.

Answer according to the concepts on the left of the rectangle:

Describe how it feels to receive your internal rewards:

Admiration
Respect
Recognition

Describe the meaning of your achievements:

A Purpose
for Living

Describe the greatest emotions matching your peak performances:

Exultation
And Triumph

Describe how you feel about your identity and integrity after a great commitment came to closure:

Identity and
Integrity

Describe how these two concepts are integrated into the Six Phases:

Freedom and
Responsibility

REWRITE YOUR DREAM STORY

Based on the Six Phases how does your story begin,
what happens next, and how does it end?

In the
beginning _____

_____

_____

_____

_____

_____

_____

_____

What happened
next _____

_____

_____

_____

_____

_____

_____

And
now _____

_____

_____

_____

_____

_____

_____

_____

Congratulations, You Have Built Your Character!

LETTING GOD BE GOD

A sentence completion exercise:

When I hear the word God…_____

My life would change if…_____

Faith is…_____

My strength is…_____

In my past…_____

Trust is…_____

My talents come from…_____

I can let go and let…_____

The stretch of glory…_____

I feel triumph when…_____

My passion…_____

The Six Phases with God…_____

I am not alone when…_____

I am on my way to…_____

Greater is he who…_____

I am complete and fulfilled when…_____

When I invite the supernatural power…_____

I reach my goals because…_____

RENEW YOUR SOUL

A free-association exercise:

☐ Your Soul contains the invisible part of your being—your feelings and your thinking.

☐ Free association means that you write down any word, sentence or image that comes to your mind when you think about the following variables: soul and goals, soul and Six Phases, or soul and ultimate success.

☐ Free association does not mean that you write down sentences that have to make sense. Jot down anything your mind releases.

☐ Write your free associations in the ornamentation below:

WHAT HAVE YOU LEARNED FROM PHASE SIX?

Give a one-sentence conclusion for the following 5 questions:

1. Your self-assessment about your Six Phases experiences:

    _____

    _____

2. Six keywords to reach your goals:

    _____

    _____

3. Rewriting your dream story:

    _____

    _____

4. Letting God be God:

    _____

    _____

5. Free associations:

    _____

    _____

SUMMARY OF PHASE SIX

Triumph in the Stretch of Glory

Write 2 or 3 ways you want to celebrate your final stretch of glory experience:

1_____

_____

_____

2_____

_____

_____

_____

3_____

_____

_____

_____

Describe how you will
TRIUMPH

YOUR FINAL ANALYSIS:
THOUGHTS ABOUT THE WORKBOOK

The primary insights I've gained about achieving my goals from this workbook are:

_____
_____
_____
_____

In the future I will stretch my self with the following method:

_____
_____
_____
_____

I am aware about building my character and I am willing to pay the following price:

_____
_____
_____
_____

I will team up with God and also with people in the following way:

_____
_____
_____
_____

ORDER BOOKS
FROM THE AUTHORS

Book: BECOME EXCEPTIONAL
Reaching Personal Greatness:
A True Life Story based on two guiding principles

Book: DO WHAT YOU DON'T WANT TO DO
Achieving Excellence as a Procrastinator

Workbook: UNLEASH THE POWER TO COMPLETE YOUR GOALS
Six Phases of awareness exercises to reach
your objectives

Seminars and
Keynote Speaking: Open to the public and to private groups

TV Appearances: By request
Consultations: Coaching and consulting for individuals and
groups in person and by phone

Order your books from:
1stBooks Library at www.1stBooks.com

1-888-280-7715

The Twin Team Inc.™

WINNING IN LIFE CONSULTATION AND SEMINARS™
Barbara Warren, Ph.D., and Angelika Drake
www.twinteam.com

ABOUT THE AUTHORS

Though identical in looks, twin sisters Angelika Drake and Dr. Barbara Warren are vastly different and complementary in character. Born in the cradle of psychology, Freud's Austria, the pair has BA degrees in Art from Florence, Italy, they fluently speak four languages, and have crisscrossed the globe many times.

Long before scuba had captured the public imagination, surrounded by dozens of sharks, Angelika was shooting twenty underwater documentaries. Meanwhile, Barbara was starring in twenty-five feature films [*I Spy, Mission Impossible*]. Together they have modeled for the biggest names in international fashion before they entered the commercial side of garment manufacture, building a network of self-run boutiques that extended as far as New York. In Mexico City they established the largest personal development school in Latin America, and taught their innovative curriculum to thousands of students for  more than fifteen years. Angelika was also a choreographer and organized some of the biggest fashion shows for thousands of people in Mexico City. Together they studied Psychology, and Barbara went on to complete her Ph.D. But still not satisfied, they took to the athletic road, literally becoming legends in their own time as they crushed record after record and set new international standards for endurance of body and mind that the layman can barely conceive of. It all could be achieved with their power to complete their goals.

Through pushing this package of improbability the pair have developed a rare wisdom and insight into techniques that motivate and keep the individual from quitting. As athletes they are unique in the world for being forerunners who push the boundaries of the baby boomer generation. They are setting an example for leadership, discipline, health, and high performance.

Practicing what they preach, the twins lives are the most dramatic demonstration of barrier-breaking and winning performances. They regularly gain full spread feature articles in high profile international media. Four books write about them, and hundreds of articles have been published in 4 different languages. They have appeared on Good Morning America, Regis and Kathy Lee, and on 120 other TV stations worldwide.

Dr. Barbara is mother to two daughters and five stepchildren. She works in private practice in San Diego, California, and has, for the past 15 years, conducted a broad variety of seminars through her company *Winning in life Seminars and Consultations*. She is married to Tom Warren, a world-class athlete and winner of the Hawaiian Ironman. Angelika is also a seminar leader and special project manager, she lives in San Diego, California, with her two sons.

www.ingramcontent.com/pod-product-compliance
Lightning Source LLC
Chambersburg PA
CBHW030359290526
45785CB00004B/1830